I'LL CRY IF I WANT TO

T0281962

I'll Cry
If I Want To

POEMS

RAQUEL FRANCO

central
avenue

2025

This is a work of fiction. Names, characters, places and incidents either are the
product of the author's imagination or are used fictitiously and any resemblance to
actual persons, living or dead, business establishments, events or locales is entirely
coincidental.

Published by Central Avenue Poetry, an imprint of Central Avenue Marketing Ltd.
www.centralavenuepublishing.com

I'LL CRY IF I WANT TO: POEMS

Trade Paperback: 978-1-77168-397-5
Epub: 978-1-77168-398-2

Published in Canada
Printed in United States of America

1. POETRY / African American & Black   2. POETRY / Women Authors

1 3 5 7 9 10 8 6 4 2

CONTENTS

To Womanhood

"I am out with lanterns,
looking for myself."

—Emily Dickinson

GOOD WOMAN

You are a good woman. Hips and thighs decorated in stretch marks like tattooed lightning bolts. Switchblade hidden in your eyeliner because going out at night alone isn't safe. You are still good, full of fury and seething teeth. You have every right to be angry. When you eat worries for breakfast you are still a warrior. When you leave the bed unmade you still have it made. People can't imagine a world without you in it, love the way you make chicken noodle soup. Whether it is made from scratch or warmed from the can, it came from your gentle hands. You are a good woman when you pop the champagne and cause a problem by having a good time. Good when you aren't afraid to turn up the volume of your own life and cause a scene. You are good when your hair is wild like brambles, your stomach soft like the flesh of a peach. You are a good woman if you are alone and build a fence around the front porch of your body. A wedding ring is not the only thing that makes a woman whole. We all came out wet and pink and screaming, but women were the only ones told to keep quiet. You: salty woman. Thick woman. Patient woman. Contrarian woman. Jawbreaker woman. Devil-trembles-at-the-sight-of-her woman. You are a good woman.

YOU CAN'T HAVE IT ALL
after Barbara Ras

but you can have strawberries
red like rubies, fat enough to take up
all the space in your cheek.
You can have swing sets waiting for your legs,
which grew up way too fast, to pump in and out
like a child's, full on joy. You can have memories
of your grandmother's hands sifting through
the cupboards to find you something
to eat even though you said you weren't hungry.
Eager to make sure you are never
empty of anything.
You can have a double rainbow appear
on a random day in April and wonder
about the hands of God. You can have summer,
the season most likely to keep its word, keep your skin
tender and sweating and craving Mama's cold
iced tea to press against your neck. You can have
hope. Tie it to your tongue, thread it with the veins
of your pumping heart, let it keep you
afloat through life's sticks and stones.
You can't have it all, but there are many
things left for your hands to hold on to.

MORNING ROUTINE

I remembered to take my meds:
tiny, sad-shaped remedies that remind
my anxiety and depression to find
another place to collapse.
Woke before the moan of the garbage truck
and my children wiping sleep from their eyes.
Brewed coffee, drowned it in vanilla oat milk.
Wrote out affirmations like "I am capable"
and "I am loving the woman in the mirror."
Read the Bible and prayed for understanding,
appreciated its silk-thin pages against the pulp of my fingers.
Walked on the treadmill for my silly
little mental health.
Felt the heat of the shower, all before 9AM.
Tomorrow might look different
but right now, I feel grounded,
my feet poised to face the hours.

I'M DONE ADULTING

Let's be mermaids.
Grow fins and befriend
bubblegum-pink jellyfish
and dolphins sharp as scholars.
Discover what it's like
for our breath to smell
of salt, for our hands to grab
fistfuls of sand from the ocean floor.
What I mean to say is,
let's get away and be
something other than ourselves.
Rent a cabin with the girls
and get drunk on giggles
and white wine.
Book a red-eye just to see
the sunset over Central Park.
Grab the closest open hand
and go dancing in the rain.
Stick our tongues out and try to catch
God's tears. Let's give these walls
something to miss and something
to talk about when we come home.

ANNIVERSARY DINNER

We're late.
We order drinks heavy with bourbon

to drown out thoughts where
we are blaming each other for our lateness.

The hostess seats us at a table smaller than
the love we used to feel for each other.

There's barely room to place our glasses,
barely room for the humming of our resentment.

The saltshaker holds all the *I love you*s
we've gone to bed without saying.

Inside the pepper grinder sit silenced seeds
of compliments we never hand out when we should.

Long-lost *I'm sorry*s flicker
in the flame of the tealight candle.

The appetizer plate lies empty of *I need you, I want you . . .*
There are a thousand words left unsaid taking up

the empty space at our dinner table.
It's so loud inside our heads and so quiet in the room,

I don't even know what we'll toast to.

TO THROW A PARTY FOR HEARTBREAK
after Mindy Nettifee

I say to heartbreak,
let's dust off the champagne flutes.
Open the windows and air out
the lingering smell clinging
to his empty side of the bed.
Let's flush the spoiled jar of love notes
down the toilet. Take the dried flowers
we've been too scared to throw away
and turn them into a crown.
Turn on Taylor and let the arches of our feet
dance the way happy people do.
Shake our tears all over the living room floor
like the breaking of a piñata.
Pour one for you and one for me, and toast.
Cheers to smashing the cake
and having it all to ourselves.
Cheers to the day we smile upon waking.
Cheers to new love on its way
to crash the party.

WHAT'S IN MY BAG

When I was young, my bag
was as large as my freedom.
I was too afraid
to leave anything behind.
Carried a tube of nude lipstick
and a slice of insecurity.
A notebook for scribbled poems
about the men who had ghosted me.
Maxed-out credit cards,
a Target gift card with a balance of 74 cents
and a loose screw. A cookies-and-cream Quest bar
to fit in my macros. Gradient blue aviators, contact solution,
a fistful of black hair ties, ibuprofen, Tums,
watermelon Trident gum, bar-tab receipts
and regrets. A pack of cigarettes and uncertainty.
A book of matches from the restaurant
where I met the love of a brief moment
in time. Now I take the risk and leave it all behind.
The arsenal in my Tupperware-sized pouch
includes my keys, debit card, homemade
organic ChapStick and no f*cks.

MY SON MET A GIRL

One he is rose-color blushing
over and has placed
on a pedestal too far from
his hands.
He worries
she does not love him.
Worries that his love is too big
to fit in her soft arms.
But Baby, I tell him,
love big!
Love like the electric
paddles that bring hearts back
to life. Love like the heroes
do in stories
with happily-ever-afters.
One day, a girl who was made to fit
inside your embrace will keep you full.
It's okay to want with your arms
wide open. It's okay to want
and not be wanted back.
God says this is where strength
learns to bench-press
our broken parts.
Take the ones who walk away
with a grain of salt,
and spill the whole shaker
of your love all over the place.

DREAM IN WHICH MY BODY IS THE SUN

I offer up rays to the mother wearing
her spouse's sweatshirt
for the third day in a row,
her children's lunch spilled down the front.

Cradle the man at the farmer's market
picking a Granny Smith apple,
his late mother's favorite,
and it feels like she is holding his hand.

Turn a 3PM thunderstorm into a sky
filled with incandescent yellow
to shine light on an old friend
I no longer call.

Warm the cheek of my husband
so he feels the love
I haven't been giving him.
Pirouette above the places where weary

legs stumble alone in the dark
and dance them back home.
I dream my body is the sun
and I do not shine only for myself.

WHEN I THINK OF SALT

I think of the earth.
How Jesus told us
we are the pinch and the sprinkle,
meant to offer up light.
To offer up love.
I think of brine
and how the ocean thickens
and thins the air
around it.
How during sunrise
the beach is littered
with slimy bubblegum jellyfish
washed up from the sea.
When I think of salt
I think of my daughter,
how we both love
these little granules
to excess. Big chunks
on hot buttered pretzels.
McDonald's golden fries
when someone has over-poured.
Crispy tortilla chips from Chipotle
dressed up in salted sequins.
In these moments,
we smile and savor
and want for nothing else.

SUMMER OVATION

Applaud fire-hydrant sprinklers
that sizzle on the hot pavement in July.
Applaud water balloons bursting
against our backs, a cool relief.
Applaud grass, green like avocados,
and the freedom it gifts
our wiggling bare toes.
Applaud being given a life
as beautiful as this.

COMPANY

This year, both kids are in school
full time. It is both a relief
and an ache. Believe it or not,
I miss their sweet chaos,
not used to this ghostly silence.
I find a My Little Pony sticker
stuck to the bottom of my toe,
an apricot-colored fox tucked
in my bed, a Pop-Tarts wrapper shining
on the coffee table.
They always leave bread crumbs
to keep me company.

A PLACE TO GO WHEN YOU NEED LOVE

Into the mouth of a poem
or the palm of a friend.
On the tree limbs of giving
when you've got nothing
left to give.
Within a child's dandelion arms
or inside a spoonful of Grandma's
homemade soup.
Sundays where there are
cozy fantasies, knit blankets
and coffee cups of comfort.
Between the whispered words
of a prayer or barbecue summers
on Dad's back porch.
Love can be found
wherever you go looking.

TELL ME YOU'RE ALONE WITHOUT TELLING ME YOU'RE ALONE

At night I dream beside the dust
on his cold side of the bed.
His toothbrush lives
in the bathroom downstairs.
When I sit down for dinner
there's always an empty seat.
We are pretenders wearing
wedding bands.
Passing shadows between
grocery store receipts, carpooling
children and never asking
how the other is doing.
We never unclench our fists
to offer up relief.
We do not kiss
each other goodnight.
I shuffle up the quiet stairs,
add one more to the thousand
sleepless nights without him.

I imagine somewhere
in the upside-down universe,
we are still entangled limbs
and mouths that can't get enough.
Somewhere, we are still in love.

SOMEWHERE

Somewhere, the pairs to our socks
haven't become snapshots
on a milk carton.
Somewhere, all dogs go to heaven.
Somewhere, we aren't in the Target aisle
stuffing red carts with things
that won't fill the void.
Instead we spend time in the backyard
with the giggles of our children.
Somewhere, we aren't missing
every beautiful thing
because we are too busy looking down.
Somewhere, there are mirrors
that only see grinning teeth
and humans who appreciate
their skin and bones.
Somewhere, we are more remedy
than destruction. We are helping
hands, and we use our hearts
as homes with welcome mats.
Somewhere, there is more
than enough love to go around.

Raquel Franco

MICHAEL, A PORTRAIT
after Sheleen McElhinney

My father is straight moonshine
bought on the side of a dusty road,
a hundred-proof bite to the throat.
He is a lazy backyard Sunday
earned after a week's hard work.
Football and a beer snug in a Koozie.
Levi's jeans, worn-in cowboy boots
and Snoop playing on the jukebox.
He is the leather smell of burning
cigar smoke winding in the open garage.
Perfect penmanship and hands
that know how to fix anything,
including Harley motorcycles
and baby-cream '69 Barracudas
reconstructed in the midnight hours.
He is a suspension bridge built
on the strength of his back, marked by calloused
palms. His fingerprints left on its cables.
He is a neon-yellow construction sweatshirt
with the arms cut off and skin that stays
burned through September.
Like steel beams and concrete pillars,
he is thick-skinned and stern enough to scare
off boys that come asking for his daughters
but soft enough to raise another man's
baby girl as his own.
The only fan in the stands
at my volleyball game.
He is not wasteful with words
but tears up on a random day

18

when he can't stop himself
from saying *I love you*.
A warm grizzly bear hug
that will always keep you safe.

NOT TODAY

The weeping alarm
breaks through the dawn.
I feel depression poke
my temple.
Take a deep inhale
and exhale, "Not today."
Today I will lasso
the sun.
Pull it in close
to warm everything
that might have grown cold.
Build a new day of joy
to sink my toes into.
Turn the shower
into a tropical waterfall.
Spray my pillow
with lavender
because this home
is a relaxing getaway.
Savor cooking
like I own a Michelin Star.
Yes, Chef. You're doing great, Chef.
Today I am building
new reasons to jump
out of bed in the morning.

If they find you terrifying,
let them be terrified.
If they say you're too much,
drown them in your muchness.
If they can't love you
for both the wonderland
and the wreckage,
then they simply don't deserve you.

BODY LOVE

If you've been avoiding mirrors,
I want you to reintroduce yourself.

Decide that your reflection is not
for counting flaws.

When you are mascara-smeared, appreciate
your eyelashes for catching the salt,

your cheekbones for rising to the occasion when
someone you love walks into a room,

your pink mouth for never keeping laughter
a secret, your shoulders for shrugging off life's

stacked bricks and never crumbling the bone.
Place your hand to your seesaw chest and say

thank you for its ongoing beat.
Thank your belly for making room

for pain and joy and big fat greasy cheeseburgers,
your thighs for rubbing against one another to keep

warm, your ankles for standing when
you lose your balance.

Stop avoiding mirrors. Your body is in relentless
pursuit of keeping you whole. Hold yourself

with both arms and say, "Thank you. Thank you
for always giving me a place to call home."

THE OLDER I GET, THE MORE I FORGET

I forget the name of my daughter
and have to list off every name in the house
just to get to the right one. "Brett! Gabe! Dog!
Cat! I mean, Penelope!"
I forget to feed the dog and wonder why
she's staring up at me with those adorable,
starved mocha eyes.
Forget anything my husband tells me to do.
Five weeks in a row I forget to buy cilantro
for the guacamole. Forget to call my brother
back. A week later, I stare at his name listed
as a missed call, and regret takes up residence
in my heavy chest. It's the last missed call
I will ever receive from him, and that . . .
I will never forget.

BABY, WHEN YOU THINK OF ME
after Daisy Jones & The Six

Baby, when you think of me,
I hope it ruins Taylor Swift,
that you see my brown eyes
whenever her songs play

in the grocery aisle, in elevators,
and on your girlfriend's lips
when she's singing in your car.
I hope it stales the hops in your IPA

and all you can remember is
the slick of my tongue
when we used to steal kisses
over cold pints at the dive bar.

I hope it ruins your bedsheets,
where we used to get lost in
the folds of our bodies for days.
I hope my scent still lingers

each time your head hits the pillow.
Baby, when you think of me,
I hope I'm always the monster
lurking underneath your bed.

I'M SORRY I CAN'T COME TO THE PHONE RIGHT NOW

I'm busy trying to find beautiful ways
to look at my body, hanging up on
words like *hate* and *disgust* and *failure*.
I'm choosing each morning to line

my mouth with patience. I'm wiping
the grime of depression off the counters,
sweeping the dust of anxious butterfly wings
from the hardwood floor. I'm working

on drawing the curtains and letting
all the light in, pulling grace from the back
of the closet and seeing how she fits.
I'm busy sorting the pieces of myself

I abandoned in a pile under the bed.
I'm turning myself from a pretender
into a version that my five-year-old self would
smile and be proud to have become.

HEARTBREAK HOTEL

The kids are at your mother's.
We're in a dusty hotel bar,
and the bartender is shouting
last call.
My high heels are dangling
from my fingertips,
and I've been dancing
to the last song for a while now.
Baby, they say it takes two
to tango, and I'm getting tired
of dancing alone.
I've got the key.
Let's head to our room.
Let's give it one last shot
and not check out before noon.

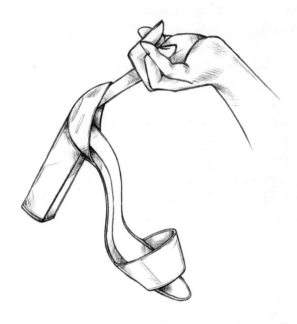

WE CAN DO IT WITH A BROKEN HEART
after Taylor Swift

To woman is an astonishing thing.
We burn both ends and still earn
degrees in between. Graduate
and show everyone just how bright
we can burn. Let the mascara running
kindle our fire and will our legs to run
marathons. Take our broken hearts to
the office. Build an altar on the corporate
ladder and climb. Hold back tears and erect
empires with our bare hands. Get no sleep
and still carve happiness inside peanut-
butter-and-jelly sandwiches shaped
like stars. Carry grief on our collarbones
and fold laundry for our families.
Smile despite getting sucker-
punched by sorrow. Smile and hold out
our arms for anyone who might need
them. Smile and heal ourselves,
little by little.

Slow, I lower my hands.
Quit begging God
for all the things I ache for
and decide
to put my palms to work.

FIFTEEN WAYS TO STAY ALIVE
after Daphne Gottlieb

1. Don't walk to the car alone during the moon's office hours.

2. Call your mother. Let her hear the sound of your voice.

3. Eat your greens. Buy yourself a fistful of flowers and bite the stems.

4. Always carry ibuprofen.

5. Keep the number to God's hotline in your back pocket.

6. Catch your grit and preserve it in the back of your throat.

7. Find people that speak your language, that sing your anthem.

8. Know that every dark hour precedes a period of light that is always worth waiting for.

9. Give. Place a twenty-dollar bill in the palm of a homeless man. Offer up your seat to the mother with tired eyes. Spill kindness on your neighbor's front lawn and see what grows.

10. Make time for your friends. Let them unload their dirty laundry in your lap then help them fold it back into place. Send them home with the aftertaste of laughter stuck in between their teeth.

11. As often as you can, say *I love you* to every person who takes up room in your heart.

12. Lose the numbers of boys with red flags.

13. Douse the photographs where you're both lovesick, his old Tupac T-shirt, the concert ticket stubs, his *Sopranos* DVD collection, all the poems. Douse them in gasoline. Light it all on fire on the front lawn. Inhale the fumes and the sweet smell of letting go.

14. Carry hope like your favorite faded Polaroid sitting in the mouth of your wallet.

15. Buy yourself champagne, and toast to every good thing you are.

Why is love so hard
and anger so big?
Shouldn't love
be the thing bigger
than any elephant in the room?

LATCH

They place her pink pixie body
in my arms. It's time to eat, little one.
Her lungs cry out, her hungry wail clawing
out space for guilt under my ribs.
I don't know what to do.
The nurse squeezes my chest like a hamburger,
shoves my breast into my baby's searching
mouth. Her gums pinch my skin like a clothespin,
but she does not drink. An hour of trying and both our faces
are red with frustration. Everyone says breast milk
will make them smart, will protect them from illness
and make me a better mother. Tears catch
in my lashes, and failure slides to my lips.
After two days without feeding, I let the nurses
give my baby a bottle of formula.
I sink into the hospital bed, terrified
that I am not going to do any of this right.
What I don't know is that my baby girl
is going to latch on to me in every way possible.
My arms will be the safety net for when her wobbly legs
trip and her face meets the pavement,
for when her cheeks flush with fever,
for when her lips tremble from life's sharp teeth.
I am the bolt, the padlock, the deadbolt
for every little thing she needs to feel safe.

SPRING BREAK SUNRISE

It's 6AM. The sun is stretching
its hands over the North Carolina coast,
painting the seagulls' wings pink and tangerine.
The ocean sighs, folds its arms
over and over onto the shore.
Dozens of jellyfish are washed up and lying
still and crystalline. The peace here is palpable,
a footprint from God Himself.
I wish the clock would stop ticking,
but two little sleeping heads
wait for me back at the beach house.
As my heels sink into the soft, cool sand,
I hope the residents here aren't taking
this backyard miracle for granted, and I wonder
what beautiful things I have yet to discover,
what's been there the whole time and I never knew it.

LOST APPETITE

We don't kiss like we used to.
Instead of making out beneath
stairwells and in parking lots,
we fold laundry with tired hands,
tuck in the children instead of each other,
take out the trash with unspoken words.
When did we become too busy to want?
When did our eyes stop being bigger
than our stomachs? When did your belly
stop growling for my lips?
Baby, aren't you starving?

THINGS I LEAVE BEHIND

Strands of hair, like confetti,
'cause everywhere I go is a party.
Cups of cold coffee I never have
enough time to swallow.
Fingerprints embedded with poetry
on every surface. Hair ties strewn
like bread crumbs. Eyelashes blown
from my fingertips as I wish
for the kind of love that offers up
its hands, wrists and elbows.
An empty wine glass from the night
before, when our laughter reached
the ceiling. Books, dog-eared, highlighted
and laid open on their bellies.
Dresses in the back of my closet
that used to know sweat and desire
and the samba of my hips. Prayers
I've painted the walls with. A telephone wire
where my love is always free
of judgment.

Lately I turn on the TV to dull
the wounds of loneliness.
Dream of smashing plates
into the hardwood floor.
Instead, I drink to swallow
the ache.

WISHES I'VE MADE WHILE TOSSING PENNIES

Please grant me an oversized porcelain
clawfoot tub to soak in until my skin wrinkles.
Give me more hours in the day to sleep, read
a fantasy series in one sitting and play
board games with the kids. For my next wish,
can my house clean itself? Add a yearly girls' trip
to a glass house in the woods, and no one can cancel.
I wish for explosions, bullets and hate that holds
triggers, to cease to exist. For every heart to feel
the lantern of God's breastbone against their pulse.
I wish for my own last supper where my mother,
my granddad, my Nother Mommy, and my brother all have
a seat at the table. I get to hear their eulogy of laughter,
memorize the twinkle in their eyes when they smile.
I get to say goodbye. I get to say
I'll always love you.

I am working on being the flower
that rose through the concrete.

BACKWARDS
after Warsan Shire

I tell the devil I am taking back the good side
of the wishbone. Pull my mother from the grave
and give the devil back his whiskey, his vodka,
his box of pink wine. Walk back into my mother's apartment,
hug her now-strong limbs, find the words
in the back of my throat and tell her I love her,
and it is not the last time. Sixteen again
and she does not chase me down the street,
her knees falling into grass. Screams are swallowed,
tears rise back up through eyelashes.
There are no grass stains. Just a kiss goodnight.
I tell the devil I am taking back the torch,
taking back the strong side of the woman
I call Mom. She puts the bottle back on the shelf,
buys her brown-eyed daughter a paperback novel
where the ending is happily ever after.
She watches me pick out my wedding gown,
tells me I am beautiful, squeezes my hand
as I push her first grandson into the world.
I tell the devil I'm taking back the moment alcohol
sank its teeth into my mother's future,
pulling apart its jaws and yanking her body
right from its mouth. I walk back into her apartment
and tell her I love her, and it is not the last time.

BARBIE GIRL

When I was a kid, my babysitter had an army
of Barbies and a bubblegum mansion
taller than my imagination.
I spent hours in their attic dressing
them up in perfect pink gowns
and placing furniture in their utopian world,
but I could never get past setting the stage.
My hands weren't for pretending.
I knew it was just an impossible hot-pink dream.
The 39-18-33 plastic doll in my small hands
didn't live in my reality. There were no blonde,
blue-eyed, perfect girls in my vanity mirror.
There were no Kens walking out of a magazine
to save a brown girl like me.
The one thing we did have in common
was that our feet weren't made
to fully touch the ground.
We were both dream girls who
weren't allowed the privilege
of wholly living.

HER BROTHER WILL ALWAYS BE THE COOLEST KID IN THE UNIVERSE

In her eager voice, all strawberries ready
to be spread onto a pb&j, my daughter asks
her brother to play. Her pink cheeks
and the slope of her sweet nose turn

toward him with anticipation.
To her he is the coolest kid in the universe,
a universe where somersaulting dragons,
roaring lions and cherry bowls of laughter exist.

His prepubescent body, caught between boy and man,
slumps in his chair, and he lets out an aggravated groan.
To him she is the shadow he never asked
to tag along. Seven years younger, she is a foreign

language to him, a bundle of clumsy arms
and legs he doesn't quite understand.
I sigh as he rolls his eyes and grunts
that he does not want to play with her.

I clench my jaw and let out
a disappointed sigh, wishing my son had
more patience in his chest.
I lament for her rejected heart,

a pink muscle yet to be cracked open.
I watch them battle back and forth,
a tug-of-war of words,
and remember that it was him who prayed

for her existence, asked God,
with his lonely and oblivious
six-year-old hands, to grant him a sibling.
Although she is not the company

he seeks in his current becoming,
he doesn't know that one day,
when all the school bus problems
fade away, she will be there. He doesn't know

that the world has a multitude of days
with salty weather coming his way,
and his sister is going to be the one
who shows up with an umbrella

and bright red rain boots.
He doesn't know that a girl is going to steal
the very oxygen from his throat and call it hers,
but his sister will be the one to remind his lungs

that a girl is just a girl and that it's time to
come up for air. He doesn't know
that when the car breaks down,
the faucet starts dripping and the hours

all catch on fire, she will have
a spare tire, a squeaky wrench
and a fire extinguisher on hand.
One day her four-year-old hands won't be too small

to hold him, her feet won't be too small
to meet him where he's at,
and as I sit on the couch waiting
for them to sort it out, I just wish

he already knew that soon there will be
no more days of pretending,
no more days with jungle gym hours
and merry-go-round minutes,

but the one thing that won't change
is the way she looks up at him,
and that no matter what he does,
he will always be the coolest kid in the universe.

Depression will steal days
and get the best of me
but so will joy.
So will joy.

HAZARD SIGNS

I want to race
with the butterflies again.
I miss falling in love with
my foot pressed to the pedal,
all hazard signs a blur
of caution-tape yellow.
Blind to the fact
that I'm heading toward
a wreckage.
It used to feel so good to hold
a heart in my hands
at ninety miles per hour.

THE LAST TIME I SAW THE GAP INSIDE HER SMILE

was before the world had been condemned
behind doors. Before we were forced to hide
our teeth and be confined to the heat of our own breath.
Now it is October 5th and she has exhaled

her last breath. I am unprepared to be six-feet-
deep away from her warm teacup presence.
I run my tongue over my sorrow, waiting
for this grief to bend at the sound of her windchime

voice saying, "Love you. See you. Bye," just the way
she always did. I grasp for vignettes of her memory
to put in my back pocket for safekeeping.
Hoping they will never rust nor fade.

Memories of my body folding into the blanket
of her arms as she whispered, "Mm, my baby."
Her kind palms clasped together with faith strong enough
to make the devil remember he too had saltwater

behind his eyes and there are women
standing on this soft earth that are to be feared.
Memories of every encouraging word she had living
inside her loveseat throat. Her long fingers, soft enough

for piano keys, building cars next to ordinary men.
Proof she never needed to rely on one.
Memories of the bone-white walls she proudly covered
with pictures of her brown-skin sons and daughters

and grandchildren and great-grandchildren.

The gap inside her tender psalm smile
that was always an altar of welcome.
She never liked her smile, never thought she was anything

to waste time looking at. Didn't know in her mouth
was the wind sweeping through two patient
curtains of comfort, a road with two yellow
lane lines that always pointed me in the right direction.

Two headlights lighting quiet prayers into the night,
and I don't know who is going to pray now
but I think it's my turn. My turn to hold on to
the same faith, white-knuckled and wanting, and to hold

our family up with *Amen*.
I hope she's listening. I hope she knows I am holding on
to the sound of her voice like a telephone cord.
Like the ceramic owls that used to perch in her living room.

I hope she is watching. I hope she knows
there was nothing more beautiful than the woman
she was and that the love her family had for her
was more than enough to fill the gap between her teeth.

Grief is no longer spooning
my spine at 3AM.

WHAT HEALING TASTES LIKE

Hope, like a half-eaten cookie
on Christmas Eve. Buttery crystal crumbs
sprinkled across the kitchen table
next to a child's handwritten letter.

Pain, like rising sourdough that's been
beaten and kneaded into submission
to birth that perfectly salted brown crust.

Time, like the ripening of a sunbaked peach
hanging from a Georgia tree, waiting
to be plucked, waiting for the juice to run.

Persistence, like bruised raspberry skin on the edge
of rotting, seduced by sugar and lemon zest
and made into jam, the kind you keep
licking off your fingers over and over again.

POEM BEGINNING WITH A RETWEET
after Maggie Smith

I don't know who needs to hear this,
but unclench your jaw.
Unfurl your brow. Stop letting
apologies roll off your tongue
so easily. Teach your mouth
the pathway toward *no*.
Instead say yes to joy, to lazy Sunday
slumbers, to getting lost
in used-bookstore aisles,
to giving your hours the chance
to meet a stranger who could change
your life. Say yes
to un-shrugging your shoulders,
to throwing your burdens in the fire,
to dancing in a storm in your best dress,
barefoot and fearless.

LOVE AND REGRET

There once was a boy.
He kissed me
in the middle of
a crowded bar,
and all the want
in the world
got tangled
in my hair.
I knew then
he would love me
then forget me,
and I would love him
then regret him.

BREATH WORK

I send anxiety a cease-
and-desist letter.
I close her mouth.
Unbind her gnawing disquiet.
Inhale for four seconds. Hold
for seven. Exhale for eight to slow
my train-track heart.
I manifest settle,
a steady river in my nerves.
I proclaim calm,
a relentless hymn on my tongue.
I end the riot in my chest
and exhale and exhale and exhale.

I THROW MYSELF A PITY PARTY

Wear yesterday's waterproof mascara
and a stream of dried salty tears.
Serve gas station Chardonnay in paper cups.
Toast to the friends who no longer pick
up the phone to ask how I'm doing.
Save the party hats for their ghosts.
Say farewell to the good old days of having
someone to spill sacred secrets to.
Twirl in the living room and shimmy
'cause no one's watching.
Write forgiveness on helium balloons
and let them float all around me.

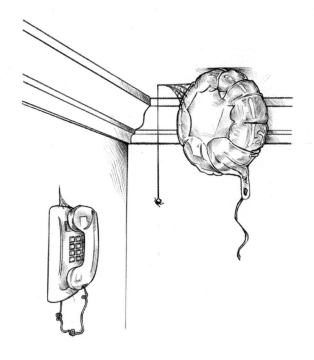

I do believe there is a way to bend grief
and turn it into something beautiful.

A BOY IS JUST A BOY
after Sam Payne

until you have stared
at his face so long his freckles become

constellations you fall asleep to.
A boy is just a boy until he leaves

you clumsy. Cups your chin in the middle
of a high school party. Kisses you with confidence

like a quarterback homecoming king.
A boy is just a boy until he walks you home.

Takes your face between his palms.
Punches you love-drunk when he whispers

I love you into the heart of your ear.
A boy is just a boy until he gives you a ring

on Christmas morning with shaky hands
and asks you to be his bride.

A boy is just a boy until he becomes a father
to your child, holds life so brand new

and skin as fragile as a pinky promise.
A boy is just a boy until he changes

everything, until he offers up
every little thing.

GOLDEN HOUR

Today there was so much light
streaming through my window,
zebra stripes glowing
past the blinds,
all I wanted to do
was bask in it and let it
clothe me in some kind of hope.

MADE IN HIS IMAGE
after Jess Janz

God said we were made
in His image, and I look
at my daughter's soft cinnamon curls
falling over her shoulder
and see God's beauty.
My son's laughter rings
through the room, and I hear
God's song. Sitting next to the Christmas tree
lights, your brown-sugar eyes twinkle,
and I envision paper lanterns floating
toward heaven. I see the soles of God's feet
as you lay yours barefoot
across my lap. I've often heard
people say God feels so far away,
but He can be found right next to us.
Folded in arms, nuzzled in collarbones,
blushing on cheeks, cradled in the hand
that reaches for mine . . .
He is everywhere.

MY DAUGHTER'S FIRST HEARTBREAK

"He said he won't marry me,"
my daughter huffs out between
broken sobs, trying to catch
her hopscotch breath. I learn
the boy next door has proclaimed
he wants to marry another
neighborhood girl.
In her devastated anger,
she pushed the girl off the
swing and came running
into the shelter of my arms.
At six years old, her world is only as big
as what she can paint with her small hands.
She has so much
yellow brick road ahead
of her to be ruined by boys.
I tell her not to waste
her treasured time looking
for love in boys with empty
vows underneath their tongues,
and arms handing out nothing
but wounds. Hope that if I keep
telling her, one day she'll understand.

NO EVIDENCE

Feels like a lifetime ago
that I loved like that.
Wanting
and wanting
and wanting.

There are no photographs.
No sweatshirts left behind.
No saved brunch receipts
or concert wristbands.

No proof that I was madly
in love with you.
We carved our names
into nothing.

My skin aches knowing
all I have left
is a fading film reel
of your smile.

NAMES I GO BY
after Michelle Awad

Peach. Spotless. No—bruised,
teetering on spoiled but still sweet.

Bitch, but the badass kind. Like
move out of the way, it's Britney
kind of bitch.

Rocky, a childhood nickname
always followed by boys yelling
Yo, Adrian!

Boo, to my husband. A word that's been
said so often it's lost its meaning.

Author, a name that is still trying
to get comfortable between my teeth
but is starting to feel right.
My tongue is making room.

IF I LIVED IN A HOUSE WITH NO MIRRORS
after Sasha Sloan

I would stop being
a tourist in my own skin,
forget all the parts
I've grown to loathe.
I'd rediscover how the yawn
of stretch marks on my hips
is a miracle. My stomach,
a temple to homemade years of living.
My thighs, a chorus
of grace. I remember my body
is a home, a holy vessel
deserving of soft words
to wash dirt from my feet.

EVOLUTION

Your twenties are for having
as many friends as you can fit
into the VIP section of a club.
For taking risks and building
a backbone. Your forties are for washing
your hands clean, letting the values
in your belly guide you. For keeping close
the ones that don't find you too heavy,
the ones that won't hang up the phone,
the ones that are okay if it's not always
just a good time.

BAD DAY

You could call this day
a shit show. Finished working,
put the key in the ignition
and my Volkswagen sighed
and took the afternoon off.
My pink *f*ck the patriarchy*
keychain nodded in the sunlight.
The dog decided the couch
was a better place to relieve herself
than the grass in the backyard,
and now it reeks of urine.
My daughter is a running
faucet of tears over having to take a bath.
Somehow, I don't panic.
I am cool as a disco.
Nothing slithers under my skin.
My bones stay poised.
Laughter escapes my lips
as I think of all the chaos.
That's some kind of growth,
I think.

SWEET SLEEP

Nine PM and the street sleeps.
The summer milk-pearled moon
hangs like a nightlight.
Here there is rest.
The tapping rain outside
my open window
gift-wraps me in comfort.
I am convinced God gifted
me that sound,
that gentle pulse,
a sweet peace for me to keep.

SUMMER BREAK

The sun is sweltering
and the kids are restless.
They call it a break,
when the buses stop running
and the teachers go on vacation,
but for us mothers
it is more of a breakdown.
It's an anxious runonsentence of days,
loud, whining mouths and tiny begging
hands at our feet. The vinyl record skipping,
"Mom, Mom, Mom, Mom, Mom, Mom."
The catalogue of our responsibilities
thickening to the size of our children growing
inch by inch. We just want to be heard.
If a mother falls in the middle
of her own living room, does she make a sound?
With *Paw Patrol* blaring, the kids' feet
thundering across the floor, the dog yapping
at the neighbor mowing the lawn, I doubt
anyone can hear us. Can you hear us?
Can you hear us breaking?

HOW TO MAKE THE MOST OF SUMMER ENDING

Pick fresh, plump tomatoes from the farmer's
market, as red as a checkered picnic blanket.

Go for a drive to nowhere with all the windows
down and let the breeze run through your hair.

Dine on a patio strung with twinkling lights,
savor a glass of wine and instead of a date, bring a book.

Build a bonfire in the backyard and roast
fluffy marshmallows.

Go to a festival, a concert, a drive-in movie
and kiss someone under the stars.

Take the kids to the park before they go off to school
to grow up without you.

I GOOGLE OLD WOMAN

and words like *dumpy*, *lonesome*,
suicidal, *gloomy*, *poor*, *crone*,
hag, and *witch* spit onto the screen.

I google *old man* and words like
distinguished, *wise*, *handsome*,
sarcastic, *talented*, *experienced*,
seasoned and *mature* appear.

My body turns on high heat
and I am all boil. I furiously
type out an email to Google:

To Whom It Obviously Doesn't Concern,

When you define *older woman*,
call us *audacious*. Call us *loved*.
Call us *silver-haired dragons*,
women who caused a riot,
*women who walked through fire
and didn't burn*. Call us *an accumulation
of laugh lines*. Call us *timeless*.
We are not cars that lose
value once they leave the lot.
Please update your search engine
accordingly, and hand her
a proper celebration.

Sincerely,
A woman who is not shrinking
with every minute she is still breathing.

I send my heart a telegram.
Tell her she won't always meet
sorrow at the front door.
The salt will wash away
and love will appear
on the porch swing,
patient and wanting.

SECRETS TO KEEP US SAFE

A memory suddenly comes into focus
with a wave of worry as I drive
to pick up my son and his friends
from the movies: I'm fourteen,

back in my grandmother's living room
sifting through worn sepia photographs,
when I find a photo of a Black man, tall
like the stems of a tripod. His face,

strong and straight-lipped, gazes back at me.
My grandmother tells me in her blanket-swaddled
voice that he is her father, my mother's grandfather.
I look into his coal-black eyes and recall the first time

I asked my mother where I was from,
where my soil had been rooted. She looked at me
with her olive skin, her Cupid's bow sharp
like the blade of a door key, and said,

"Just tell people you are Hispanic."
She did not tell me the blood braided in my veins
was also Black. Every summer when I'd run
my undeveloped legs through the front lawn sprinklers

or swim in the backyard baby pool, my mother would slather
me with SPF 50 sunscreen. The one in the pink bottle
where the bare-chested little girl is getting her underwear
pulled by a dog. My mother would then bark at me,

"*Don't get too dark!*" I'd stare at my skin, brown like the edges

of an old Polaroid, and wonder why that was a bad thing.
It made the feet of my chest pace.
My grandmother took a deep breath and prepared herself

to spill secrets she'd been cradling close to the chest.
Explained that when my mother was deep in her girlhood,
the neighborhood girls would straddle her fragile young body
and use their fists to try beating the melanin right out of her.

Like the scar above her perfectly arched eyebrows that she inherited
from their hands, my mother's skin was a civil war.
My eyes shut tight as I realized why she taught me that *kinky*
was a word you never wanted your hair described as.

Why we spent hours in the bathroom straightening
out my tight curls with a hot comb. The room smelling like a bonfire
of secrets, burnt-hair smoke swirling as the comb hit my black tendrils.
My knees shaking as time passed, but I didn't ask questions

because all I wanted was to be as beautiful as her.
My mother had been a secret keeper, in a dark room
collecting negatives from our family scrapbook she never wanted
developed. She had been playing pretend, dressing up

the filter of my skin to look like something safe to touch,
something safe when exposed to a room full of white faces,
and now, twenty-five years later as I pull up to the front of the theatre,
I worry that my own child, whose complexion pales next to my own,

will be judged by his mother's pigmentation. Am I about to understand
more deeply why Mother felt that our family tree was a secret to keep?

DANCING IN THE KITCHEN

and our kitchen is better
than any ballroom.
I grab the milk.
You cup my waist,
stir me across the room.
We forget the need for pancakes.
Leave the pan hot and sizzling
on the stove.
In the dawn of the refrigerator light,
our laughter whisks into jam
and you satiate my sweet tooth.
In this moment, I know I am ready
to spend all my small
eternities with you.

FIRST CHILD

You're getting ready for your first high school dance,
straightening your thin black tie. You ask me how
to tuck in your shirt, and I laugh. Fourteen is like having
thick baby legs and learning to walk all over again.
Watching you chat with your friends, my eyes swim
with pride as carefree joy breezes off your shoulders.
I think back to that day in your father's bathroom, waiting
for test results my gut already knew.
As I bit my fear and chipped nails down to the beds,
the verdict of two red lines appeared like a magic trick.
Damn it hissed through my teeth as I slammed
the shotgun stick in the sink.
It's not that I didn't want you. I just wasn't ready for you.
Twenty-seven and still learning to pay bills on time.
Learning to love in all the right ways. Trying to discover
who I wanted to be in this big, big world. I didn't know yet
that the answer was you. Your perfect tiny fingers and toes,
a quiet psalm on my chest, awakened my dormant mother tongue.
Gave me soft eyes to see a world outside my own. To know love
like milk braided with honey.

IT'S MY BIRTHDAY

and I'll cry if I want to.
Cut the cake with my bare hands.
Jam a whole slice in my mouth like
a groom feeding the bride.
I am the bride.
I lick pink icing off my fingertips and do not say
I'm sorry.
There are no apologies,
only thank-yous.
Thank you for the years threaded with arms
that said *I love you* and meant it,
for jaw-wide-open laughter,
words that gave me a home I could write myself into,
for allowing me to answer to two sets of small
tugging hands calling me Mama.
I say thank you to depression and anxiety
for showing me that I am some kind of magic,
stronger than I ever thought possible.
This year is for smiling with all my teeth and telling
the woman in the mirror I love her. I'm proud of her.
This year I will blow out forty candles and make
only one wish . . .
for more and more and more love.

PURPOSE

You are a beautiful thing
even when you are broken.
Even when you feel too tired
to find reasons for all this
not-so-tender living.
There is a story inside
your fingerprints
that you have yet to unfold,
that someone
still needs to hear.

I HAVEN'T MET THE ME YET

that doesn't sit quiet in the driver's seat
as her friends laugh and call her a white girl
when her brown skin says otherwise.
I haven't seen the version that doesn't let
white faces tell her they are more Black
than her or that she doesn't know racism.
Haven't met the one who doesn't cower
at the man arguing with her at a gas station,
telling her she is Filipino after she politely
tells him she is not.
I haven't met the version of me
that doesn't feel uncomfortable walking
into a room full of white women or Black women
because I am neither and I am both.
I think it's time to meet her,
to cut the noose from her tongue
and claim the salsa in her blood,
the tribe, the collard greens
and the fifty stars.
It's time to speak up and let the world
know no one gets to tell me who I am
or where I come from.

KELLY CLARKSON SAID, "IF YOU'RE GONNA THROW SH*T, THROW DIAMONDS."

Toss kind words around like glitter
at the stroke of midnight on New Year's Eve.
Let your voice shine like a mirror ball.
Throw your arms around the bodies
of those who have given up space
to love you. Throw meaningful *I love you*s
around as often as the sun rises,
because you never know what day
will be the last. Throw dandelion crowns
on doorsteps to remind others to keep
on wishing for every good thing
they can imagine.

PORTRAIT OF A SUNDAY

Yes, there is a pile of toys
at the bottom of the steps
that need put away.
Clean laundry in the basket
waiting for its hangers.
A sad-eyed dachshund begging
for treats and needing a bath.
Kids on their iPads that need
my undivided attention.
Life is always waiting
but today, today I will wear the day
like my Sunday best,
like there is nothing in
my bones I should be
apologizing for.

ACCEPTANCE

I no longer exist only to be
wanted. That world is for
your youth. Now I am settling
into a slower body. Like moving
into a new home, I am adapting
to the creaks and moans of its
bones. I am watching my hair,
black as pepper seeds, be taken
hostage by the unforgiving hands
of time. My crown left with salt
I can't shake out. I am accepting
the wrinkles carving their way
around my eyes as proof
of tender memories
instead of a countdown.

NOW THAT WE DON'T TALK

Losing a friend is like growing a phantom limb.
A ghost of you sits at the Friendsgiving table.
I spot a Grace and Frankie card on Galentine's Day,
and an echo of your laughter billows through the store.
On the Fourth of July, the memory of your tambourine voice rings
louder than fireworks. Moments of amnesia
have me reaching for the phone to talk about things
only we cared about, like the best shampoo to stop
your hair from falling out or Sandoval cheating on Ariana.
When I lose my brother, the phone waits, breathless, for your call.
I put on all black and salt the pews with my tears,
my hand empty of yours as they read his eulogy.
I say goodbye to him on Instagram. Our text thread keeps
collecting dust. I get the type of news I can cross off
my bucket list, and you're the first person I think to tell.
You would've been there to smash champagne flutes
and spill joy on the floor with me. People ask
how you are doing and I answer, with awkward lips,
that I do not know. It is strange to no longer be a witness
to your life, which used to be so intertwined with my own.
Nobody talks about how to hold this type of heartbreak
in your hands. I don't know how to close the wound.
I am an idle body with a gaping hole in the company
of my heart, one half of a broken best friend charm.

SLOW GIRL SUMMER

Build a bucket list that needs no cellphones.
Get more acquainted with the blood orange
face of the June sun. Throw the soft fabric
of your skin into a lake. Fold your body
like a baby in the womb and cannonball
yourself into the deep. Let there be more happy
hours, the sweat of a glass dripping down
your wrist on a patio with a string of starry lights.
Take yourself to a strawberry garden and stain
your fingertips ruby red. When it rains, stroll
the aisles of an old bookstore and strum
the spines of stories yet to be ventured into.
Lose time's phone number. Slow dance
through summer to the percussion
of your own pulse.

WILD CHASE

I just wanted someone
to chase the wild with.
Meet me at Mirror Lake.
Surrender our clothes
and jump in toes first.
Lie on soft blue grass
and confess our sins
to a litany of stars.
Jump in your pickup truck,
get lost on winding roads
under a canopy of autumn leaves.
Drain the bank account
and wake up
slow dancing in Central Park.
Chase all the wild
we could ever imagine.

Love has not always been
kind to me. I have survived
a thousand small deaths,
but love is still the thing
worth living for, is still reason
to answer when it calls
you home.

PINK IS MY POWER COLOR

like Victoria's Secret pink underwire
doused in gasoline and burning
on the front lawn.
Like sweating-in-a-glass lemonade pink
I made from scratch,
the pulp of summer lemons
and crushed ripe raspberries smudged
on my fingers.
Like peony buds from Trader Joe's
that will bloom
just in time for dinner to be served.
Pink like taste buds, the howl on my tongue
I won't keep quiet.
Pink like *Burn Book*, where I keep
all my dirty-mouth secrets lined
in a lipstick called Orgasm.
Pink is a girlhood city like Barbie, like ballet
slippers, like strawberry milkshakes
and Bubblicious bubble gum.
Pink is my womanhood kingdom
like Panther, like jellyfish sting,
like Natalie Portman's gaze in *Closer*,
like salt, like taffy, like whatever
the hell makes me happy
and includes the color pink.

WAYS IN WHICH I HAVE WITNESSED GOD

At first it felt like alchemy.
My mother would hold my unsure hands
and pray with me. Ask God to answer
my small-girl dreams, like making
the cheerleading squad. My finger trailed down
the list, but my name wasn't there.
My mother said *keep praying*
and wouldn't you know, a girl moved away
and her spot became mine.
My mother's faith was unfailing.
At a birthday party, my baby brother
plunged down the stairs in his walker.
Fear gripped our throats but not my mother's.
She scooped him up, spilled prayers from her sharp
tongue and healed the injuries right off of him.
There wasn't a scratch
on his chubby, fragile body.
My grandmother's faith was just as steadfast.
Anytime I was about to get on a plane,
her name would appear on my phone screen.
We'd catch up while I paced before the gate,
and then she'd say a quick prayer for my safety.
I never told her I was going anywhere. She just
knew. When my children were plum-sized
embryos somersaulting in my belly,
I sent up so many requests to Him.
Each day they grow, I see them answered,
from my son's height to his awe-inspiring
intelligence. For my daughter, I asked
that she bring joy into the world, and she
makes me laugh like all the cherries on top.

Every day, I am in awe of answered prayers,
and I look forward to witnessing more.

THANKSGIVING

Your brother kisses his wife
while she mixes the mashed potatoes.
Tells her she looks beautiful.
She waves him off,
asks him not to make everyone sick.
But what I wouldn't give for a kiss
in the middle of the kitchen.
For you to say anything that meant
I was something to be thankful for.

Raquel Franco

A LIST OF THINGS I'M LETTING GO

People who tell me I am a thing
that is too heavy for them to carry.

Friends who only speak
to me in group chats and invite
me to girl dinners just to snap
photos for Instagram.

Guilt, for when my sacrifice
is out of balance and I offer
goodnight kisses on sleepy cheeks
instead of bedtime lullabies,
so Mama can write furiously
through the night.

Rage escaping my throat
when my children are climbing
and clawing and closing their ears
to hearing me.

The swirling glass of wine
at night to ease the humming weight
of stacked responsibilities upon
my shoulders.

Trying to forge myself into anything
and everything perfect all at once.

Whatever doesn't help me feel
lighter and more like love.

GIRLS' NIGHT

Girls' night out used to be
for wrapping our bodies
in leather and low-cut silhouettes.
Anything to catch the gaze
of a dive-bar boy that we'd try to turn
into a husband. Shots of Patrón,
cigarette smoke and dancing by the moon.
We were lightning in a bottle, living.
Now we drink wine and make reservations
for 6PM. Whisper confessions of how we hate
picking up our husbands' day-old dirty clothes
off the bathroom floor. Admit we are losing hair
from our girlhood and gaining gray ones
from raising our children. We laugh,
and still we share something
only we can understand.

POET BARBIE

Barbie wears pink from the bow
of her lips down to the arches
of her feet and hopes she will be
considered a serious artist.

She writes poems about plastic
and how it is always associated
with money and how her body is nothing
but a thing people want to buy.

Barbie wears a smile as wide
as the arms of all the Kens that do not love her.
Writes revenge poems about them
alone in her Malibu Dream House.

She takes late-night drives, shoves her heel
to the pedal of her baby-pink convertible Corvette,
lets a song about a cruel summer take the passenger seat
and lets the wind convince her she is flying.

For Barbie, the sand in her hourglass
is never running out and neither are the poems.
She knows there is so much more to write about
than boys with dimples who are always leaving.

She watches the wounds of the world
and finds beautiful metaphors inside them.
She sculpts words into a place where the world can sit
on the front porch of an ordinary dream and believe in it.

UNREAD

Every June, surrounded
by candles
and the fluttering flame
of possibilities,
I always wish
I'll hear from you.
But this year
I'm tired
of waiting
on broken-promise love letters,
so when you leave
your breadcrumb *Happy Birthday*
in my inbox . . .

I do not answer.

WHERE ARE THEY?

Where are the fathers that stay, with arms
like a deadbolt that will never break open?
Arms to teach girls what safe tastes like.

Where are the men that hunt for
forever, not just the time it takes to see
what mysteries are underneath her clothes?

Where are the men that stand up
for all the fathers' daughters?

Where are the men who don't hold fake promises
under their tongues, the ones who don't hide
wolf snarls behind sheep's grins?

Where are the ones that leave trust
on her pillow, and doors she can leave
unlocked while she dreams?

TRUTHS ABOUT DEPRESSION

We forget to call back our mothers, and they worry that we do not
love them.

Invitations to dinners, coffee dates and crowded rooms are envelopes
of hope we wish we could RSVP to.

Rock bottom is a place we visit often. We've left our toothbrush, a hair tie
and an old T-shirt stained with the color of sadness. We might move in
soon.

We are a straitjacket of things undone. The carpet is a slumber of clothes
we can't put away. The dishes we ate off when happiness kept us full
sit spoiling in the kitchen sink. Shampoo begs to touch our sour scalps.

2AM antidotes are never at the bottom of a liquor bottle or a vial of pills
melting in our stomach lining. We try to pour into what's empty,
but there's always a leak, and sometimes we drag ourselves to the grave
trying to satiate the blues singing in our chests.

When we say we are fine, we mean the only thing protecting our pulse
is knowing we can close our eyes and go back to sleep, even if that means
missing payment due dates or our sister blowing out thirty lit candles,
or our child's bubblegum-sticky embrace, or the possibility of joy getting
stuck in our smile.

We try therapy. Sit on the couch with too many pillows and try to unfold
our rusted trauma. A father who's never home in time to say
grace. A mother who used wooden spoons to teach us a lesson.
A classmate who thought it was their right to slip their hands up
our skirt. A neighbor who stole our body from us when we were too young
to scrape the word "no" from our tongues. These are not excuses

but the things that punched our brain and altered its chemicals.

People with glasses half full of serotonin do not understand. They all want us to get over something we are trapped under, but this is more than just melancholy. It is a suicide note that we're trying not to put onto paper for our family members to find.

We dip our hands in a candy jar of Tic Tacs with names like Lexapro, Prozac, Zoloft and Wellbutrin. Side effects may include insomnia, fatigue, blurred vision, and thoughts of necktie nooses that make us wonder why we are taking pills in the first place, but we must.

The only thing we know is to hope. Hope as thin as a mountain of Kleenex tissues, that can only be climbed by putting one foot in front of the other. Swallow the pills. Step. Visit your therapist's office. Step. Take the shower. Step. Call your mom. Step. These small steps add up to make us feel some kind of happiness, feel anything but all this dark.

Lately, I am a dwindling wick,
burning and burning
and burning all the time.

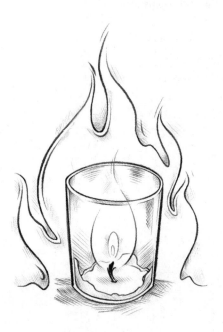

BUT GOD

I have seen God spin
hopelessness into a miracle,
so who's to say we can't fall
back in love.
Find ourselves tugging
at each other's clothes,
your boozy tongue tracing
my collarbone. Who's to say
we can't be a team, two heads
bent in a huddle, exchanging ideas
instead of sorrow.
So the next time our voices rise
above our solemn vows,
I will return to my room,
and inside the radio static
I will whisper,
But God . . .

I'M SORRY I'M LATE

I never used to be late,
always the first guest to the party,
drinking alone as I waited
for an apologetic friend across town.

This was before husband, before sharing a bed
and priorities we're both trying to squeeze
into the same hours. Before child number two,
another set of tiny reaching arms vying

for my attention, begging me with tearstained
strawberry cheeks not to leave.
Before the house, and rooms that are never not littered
with dirty socks, children's library books,

random empty Tupperware bowls and my anxiety
spilled all over the hardwood floor.
Before I was a stay-at-home mom whose time
gets lost between the cushions along with

Pop-Tarts crumbs and Lego pieces. Before this,
all I ever wanted was a groom
to fill my midnight hours,
sharing whiskey and secrets and rooms

that held laughter. All I ever wanted
was little hands to hold and bedtime stories to read,
lullabies to sing into their necks while their eyes
closed to dream. All I ever wanted was a place

that tasted like home, the days of changing my address
gone, a house that stood still. So, dear friend
who is waiting for me at the restaurant across town,
I'm sorry I'm late. I haven't quite figured out

the seesaw of all that interrupts me when I am trying
to get dressed or find the keys or text back
that I am on my way, and when those eyes
look up at me and ask for one more

hug or one more kiss or one more story
that all add up to worthy minutes spent,
I can't help but give them away.

ON DAYS I HATE MY BODY
after Joy Sullivan

I remember the fleshy pink
color of my lungs rising and falling.
My favorite lace dress that I think God
stitched with His holy hands
just for me to feel beautiful in my bones.
My rose-colored taste buds
that are lucky enough to swim
in blueberry-lavender almond lattes
and greasy New York–style pizzas.
A fresh bruise that, if I didn't exist,
would never get the chance to heal.
My ribs for caging a wild heart like mine.
One that swings like a pendulum
from wanting to hold everything
like a closed fist, to letting everything
fall and fend for itself.
On days I hate my body,
I am just thankful
I'm alive.

WHEN MY DAUGHTER GETS HER PERIOD, I WILL TELL HER HER PERIOD IS A BAD BITCH

She doesn't care who might be trying to tiptoe
his way into your underwear. *Let them see.*
Let them see the copper howl, maroon stain.
You are a woman. Paint the town red.

When you say you are on your period and men mumble
"*gross*" under their breath, she gets cranky. Grows sharp teeth,
bites their ignorant hands. She knows there is nothing
disgusting about your superpower, one that bears

beautiful children and gives life to the men whose appetites
are cramped by the iron of your sacrifice.
She will never let you settle for a lover who won't smile
at blood on the sheets. Smile when you ask him to buy the tampons.

She does not ask permission to show up at the party,
and when you find yourself without your plastic-tube armor,
and sweat beads at your forehead, she whispers,
Do not coil into yourself. Do not mourn the fabric

of your ivory dress. Stand up straight like men
do in their three-piece suits. Shows you how to wear
the five extra pounds like you're bloated
on a revolution. Takes your mood swings and twirls them

like the hands of a biological clock. Refuses to let you wipe
your fickle tears that flow for babies on TV screens.
Appreciates the tenderness of your breasts, still soft
like when a girl is first born. She will teach you that the pit

of your body should not be seen as punishment.
You own the cherry. Create a noose out of the stem.
Decide that no one will make you feel
shame for the siren between your legs.

CAR THERAPY

Some small gifts look like sitting in the parking lot,
where calm lays the blanket of its body
over your shoulders. Where white-knuckled gripping
the steering wheel, scream-singing
"Who's Afraid of Little Old Me?" releases all the rage.
Turns the bubble of your own four doors into a solo
concert. Where joy is going to the drive-thru unencumbered,
ordering a large Dr Pepper and letting the fizz tickle
your nose. Where the driveway is a safe space to avoid
going inside where the kids are loud as tambourines.
Where tears are welcome and it's encouraged to throw
a pity party. The only dress code requirements here are
salted cheeks, red rims and the freedom to spill
sadness onto the dashboard. Where the breeze keeps
you company. Windows down, driving beneath the moon's
pearling heels when no one else is around.

ALL THE WAYS TO SAY I LOVE YOU

Grab my ass in front of the kitchen sink,
so I can wet your wanting face
with my foamy hands and plant
my lips on you.

Tell me I am beautiful when the night
has done its worst and my skin
is bare and vulnerable. Whisper it
into the yawn of my collarbone.

In every crowded room,
find the small of my back.
Let me feel the grip of your fingertips
telling me you're mine.

Kiss me on the sidewalk
like I am the protagonist of a rom-com.
Hand at the back of the neck,
thumbs tracing the alcove of my cheekbone.

Curl your body around my bones like a spoon
on days depression sinks its teeth in.
Offer up grace, offer up patience,
offer up space for me to be imperfect.

GORGEOUS, GORGEOUS GIRLS

wear red lipstick to coffee shops just to leave a mark,
sequins to bed so the whole room shimmers,
and oversized sweatshirts on first dates because their bodies
are not the thing meant to be on display.

Gorgeous, gorgeous girls learn to love themselves
gently like a helping hand. Let the word "No"
carve out a home in their mouths. Know heartbreak
shatters a little softer when you decide
to hold your worth close to the chest.

Gorgeous, gorgeous girls cry and have anxiety
and carry open wounds
but still build cities that will be named after them.

Gorgeous, gorgeous girls have soft bellies.
Dance in kitchens. Laugh and howl with other girls
and don't care how much their skin shakes
when they do it.

Gorgeous, gorgeous girls believe in love
no matter how many times they've felt the impact
of love's drunk punch. Take the long way home,
blast Taylor Swift so loud even the birds believe
love is something worth returning to.

THIS IS FORTY

Having the balls to say I am forty. In a poem.
For everyone to read.

The way my mouth turns up and my hands clasp
together with joy at the thought of buying
a new vacuum cleaner.

Returning to my first love: books. Pressing
my nose into the spine and inhaling adventures
I'm running out of time to live.

Becoming softer in every way. My belly a fruit bowl
of ripe peaches. My tongue a dulling edge
that I can sharpen if I need to.

Letting God in.
His worn hands wet with clay as He places my heart
on the potter's wheel.

Dancing in the kitchen. My hips a disco ball
spinning in the afternoon light.

Walking to the bus stop wearing yesterday's
sweatpants. My hair a bramble of sleep held
hostage by little bodies climbing into bed after
a bad dream. My daughter hugs me goodbye
and loves me anyway.

Dream chasing. When I'm eighty and golden lines
are burrowed in my skin, I hope I am still running
toward some impossible dream.

ACKNOWLEDGMENTS

First, I want to give thanks to God. Without Him, I don't know where I'd be. I prayed for this book. I am blessed to have been answered.

Thank you to my children, Gabriel and Penelope. I love your guts! You have helped me become the woman that I am today. You are my world.

Thank you to Central Avenue for this opportunity and for believing in this book. To Michelle, thank you from the bottom of my heart for your incredible patience. To editors, Jessica and Molly, thank you for your incredible work and input. I appreciate you all.

Dear Reader, I thank you for being here. It is an honor. I hope you found peace, hope and a little courage for your journey, and I thank you for being a part of mine. Never stop using your voice and loving and striving to be a better version of the incredible person you are.

Raquel Franco is a multi-racial poet of Venezuelan descent living in Ohio. She is the author of *I'll Cry If I Want To* and *When the Bee Stings* and her work has been featured in *Thought Catalog* and *Rattle*. When she is not reading, writing or keeping up with two kids she is listening to Taylor Swift.

@raquelfranco.poet